She Has A Big 'But'!

Get Past Your Excuses & Realize Your Dreams

Jean Bailey Robor

First Edition

ISBN: 1453898611
ISBN-13: 978-1453898611

Cover Design & Layout by J

Author Photo: FlashbacksByRed.com

www.shehasabigbut.com

Published in the United States of America
Celebrate Life! Publishing

She Has A Big 'But'!

For Ray, Bailey & Becca who love me despite my Big 'But'!

She was accomplished, successful and everyone knew it. Then he leaned over to me and said, "She has a big but." In fact, she had several. She had overcome them all to be here, in this moment.

CONTENTS

Introduction

Excuses, excuses!

Are you bombarded with excuses to fail?
I know I am!

It's often the choices we make and the situations we find ourselves in that make all the difference from living a life we love to spiraling into an abyss of self-destruction. From the little things to the most impossible, our big 'buts' can easily get in the way of living a fulfilling life.

In *She Has A Big 'But'!* you'll find women from all walks of life who had every excuse to fail yet found a way to succeed. From the woman who was sexually abused as a child to the woman who, after doctors labeled her child as 'incurable,' worked relentlessly to find a cure...you'll find courage rise from weakness, confidence rise from uncertainty, success rise from failure.

This book is a tribute to the women whose lives are chronicled here. You'll find their stories both powerful and revealing as you rejoice when they overcome life-changing obstacles and get their big 'buts' out of the way. Their voices will not only echo on these pages but will echo within your heart as you reach for your own dreams.

What about you?
Do emotional barriers in your life keep you from realizing your dreams?
Do you fear your past experiences will prevent you from reaching your greatest potential?
Does success often seem unachievable?
Does your past dictate your future?
Do you have every excuse to fail?

Do YOU have a big 'but'?

In the following pages you'll find out how these women found success despite their big 'buts.' As you read, it's my hope that you'll be inspired and realize that you, too, can find the same success, the same victory, the same joy.

Don't let your big 'but' get in the way of your dreams!

Jean Bailey Robor

Jean Bailey Robor

CHAPTER 1
JENNY'S STORY

Jean Bailey Robor

"*Everything you want is on the other side of fear.*"

Bailey Allard, President, Allard Associates, Inc.

oday I celebrate life. Yesterday, not so much. I had gone to my doctor's office for a routine physical. I was a bit overdue. I've never really liked going for a physical, especially when I feel fine. So, I tend to put it off. This year was no exception. In fact, I felt so good, so healthy; I almost called and cancelled my appointment. I mean, my work was really busy (I'm an accountant and the office was short staffed) and I really didn't want to take time away from the office. Another excuse to avoid the appointment. But something prompted me to keep it. It's a good thing I did.

Everything went like clockwork until the breast exam. I saw a look of concern, almost imperceptible, cross the doctor's face. She felt something. Then I felt it. A lump. It was rather small but I knew that size did not matter. I felt bad that I had missed it. Then again, it had been awhile since I'd done a self examination.

That day, back at the office, my mind was not on my work. Tests had been scheduled and I was anxious. I felt a sinking feeling within my heart. But I held onto hope. Just a few short years before, I'd had a lump. It turned out to be fluid-filled and benign. In his office, the doctor aspirated it and that was that. Still, I was nervous, but hopeful that this situation would have the same outcome.

Instead, what the tests revealed would change my life forever. Cancer. The big 'C.' I had known women who had been diagnosed with breast cancer. Two were survivors; one had died. I felt so alone.

The diagnosis came near Christmas. I wasn't sure if I should tell my family or wait until after the holidays. But I felt so alone. No one, not even my husband, knew about the tests. I had been clinging to the hope that it was all some sort of mistake, that the tests would reveal nothing, that the lump was some kind of benign abnormality. Now that reality was sinking in, I knew I could not go it alone. I needed some support. I needed my family.

While the children were at school, the last week before winter break, I broke the news to my husband, Dean. Stunned, he sat beside me on the bed, holding me, quiet, as tears ran down both our cheeks. Later, he would admit he'd been scared to death; several of his family members had died from cancer.

> "I knew I could not go it alone."

Less than a month from discovering that little lump, I was scheduled to have my right breast removed, a mastectomy. Coming to grips with losing my breast was not easy but the support of my husband and family made it bearable. The surgery went well. Still, just to make sure all the cancer cells were gone, I would have to undergo 4 months of chemotherapy. That was the hardest part.

Chemotherapy is a treatment where powerful drugs are used to kill off cancer cells. Because the drugs are so powerful, there are side effects; some are mild but others can cause serious complications. In my case, chemo caused me to lose my hair. It also caused extreme nausea, every few days when I would take a treatment.

Some days I didn't know which was worse, looking like death or feeling like it. Caring for my family was impossible. That put the burden on Dean, who rose to the challenge. But I was miserable.

I tried to keep a positive attitude, but it was difficult to be positive when I was puking my brains out. Still, I kept telling myself, this could not last forever. There were times when I was so sick, and I wanted it to end so badly, I would have welcomed death.

After the chemo treatments were over, I visited my doctor. This time I didn't go it alone. I took Dean with me. As she looked into my eyes, I felt Dean's arm tighten around my shoulders. This was not just my life in the balance. This was his life, too, and the lives of our children. Whatever she said, good or bad, would affect us all. When we heard the verdict, the tears flowed down both our cheeks again. But this time, they were tears of joy! No cancer, she'd said.

It was gone!

Yesterday, I feared death. But today, like many other breast cancer survivors, I celebrate life.

Yesterday, I didn't understand what a cancer diagnosis means to a family. Today, I do. Last year, with the help of family and friends, I was the top fund-raiser in my local Relay for Life[1]. Yesterday, life hung in the balance. Today, life is good. And if you see me around, chances are I'm the one in the pink t-shirt that reads: *Save the Ta-tas!*

---

[1] An event designed to celebrate survivorship and raise money for cancer research.

Her Big But:

Jenny felt very alone and had every reason to give up with her cancer diagnosis but instead, she bravely endured surgery and chemo. She didn't let her big 'but' get in the way; her breast cancer experience led her to fight for others who face the same devastating diagnosis every day.

What can you do today to help someone else who is facing health challenges?

Jean Bailey Robor

CHAPTER 2
SHARON'S STORY

"Celebrate today.
Celebrate who you are and what
you have to offer. Celebrate your
potential today."

Mike Geffner, journalist

$\mathbb{D}$o you consider yourself ugly? Do you consider yourself flawed? Do you wish you could have a perfect life like the superstars you see on television and in the movies?

Imagine having those who you trust reinforce your negative impressions of yourself. Sure, their intentions might be well-meaning, but look at the effect of living in this kind of environment. Perhaps they are trying to keep you humble, preventing you from becoming too "full of yourself" and becoming disappointed to find that you are just a common person... nothing special... just ordinary.

Welcome to my world as a little black girl growing up on the Southside of Chicago, Illinois when black was just starting to be beautiful. My grandmother was old school because in her reality, the white man was the only smart person and the white woman was the epitome of beauty. She struggled through life raising her two daughters and soon after, her husband left her for another woman.

Through her bitterness she imbued her sense of helplessness and disappointments into her youngest daughter, my mother, and me.

Peaches, her nickname since childhood, became Ma Peaches to me and my sisters. She worked tirelessly as a maid and housekeeper, sometimes working 60 hours a week. She had to take the bus to and from her patrons' luxurious homes. When she got home late at night, she carried her tired body into the family's apartment with bags of groceries. She considered it her lot in life to suffer and wanted to protect her children and grandchildren.

Protection meant ensuring we didn't upset the "white folks." She would often tell me, "The white man is always right. Whatever you do, don't step out of line." One would think we lived in the Old South, but this was Chicago,

Illinois: a supposed safe haven after the civil war. But Chicago was in actuality one of the most racist cities in America. Plus, we had to deal with the mob.

When I was about six years old, I remember vividly hearing a succession of gun shots outside of our second story apartment. I ran to the window, followed by my mother, grandmother, great-grandmother, and those who lived in our large apartment (to help share the rent). I saw Mr. Alexander, our landlord, lying on the street with blood coming from his chest. Incredulous, I watched as a long, sleek black limousine peeled rubber and sped away.

My great-grandmother and Ma Peaches looked at all of us solemnly and whispered, "No matter what happens, y'all didn't see anything. You understand?"

I was perplexed. We heard the shots, saw the limousine, and saw the three white men who scurried into the limousine after the shooting.

How come we couldn't say anything?

The police and detectives knocked on our door a few hours later. "Remember," Ma Peaches whispered, "You saw nothing!"

> "How come we couldn't say anything?"

It was years later that I realized that Ma Peaches was protecting us. I learned that if we had related anything that we'd seen, our lives would have been in danger.

Knowing that she was right, I trusted Ma Peaches' judgment. After all, she was right about Mr. Alexander's murder, wasn't she?

As I blossomed into a young girl, Ma Peaches set upon me to protect me from becoming too sassy and self-confident. She'd say, "We always have to remember our *place*." This thinking manifested itself into my never expecting to amount to much in life.

I overheard her talking on the telephone one day to one of her friends. "Yes, the girls are growing like weeds. Sharon is the plain one, not much to look at."

It was a knife through my heart. I never thought of myself as attractive, but to hear that I'm "not much to look at" deflated any pride I had in thinking I was special.

(She did say I had a good personality, but that didn't mean much to me at the time.)

To add to my being humble, my sisters and I attended weekly a church that taught us it was:

- o Sinful to dance
- o Sinful to look at ourselves in mirrors
- o Sinful to be prideful
- o Sinful to wear makeup
- o Sinful to kiss without being married

So, how could I possibly set goals for myself when I had so much working against me?

My father despised my grandmother because of her influence on my mother and me. But he was helpless to teach me another way of thinking. To make matters worse, he was accidently killed when I was twelve years old. Ma Peaches moved in with us and ruled with an iron fist.

To add to my woes, before my father's death, I suffered from another traumatic episode when I was eight years old.

One of my grade school buddies invited me to her house. She said her mother was going to prepare lunch for us. I could hardly wait! I arrived at her house the next day, surprised when my friend gave me a scornful look. She said her mother was upset because she didn't realize her daughter was bringing a 'n-----' to their house. *What?* Now, I was really confused and unhappy. I'd lost one of my best friends only because of the prejudices of her mother.

My grandmother took me to the doctor years later to figure out why I bit my fingernails to the quick. The doctor said I had a case of nerves and prescribed pills.

Now that I've told you how my developmental years were so warped, let me now explain what happened in my life to transform me from that scarred little black girl to the successful executive woman I've become.

The answer is education and corporate America. IBM was hiring in the marketing and education departments. Although I was a secretary (now known as Administrative Assistant), our computer repairman told me that he thought I had the kind of personality IBM was looking for. Well, Grandma did say I had a good personality. I had no college degree, dressed in an unprofessional manner (super short skirts, funky shoes and jewelry), but decided I'd take a chance.

What did I have to lose? The curse of my childhood made me want to strive for a better life. I bought new professional clothes, said a prayer, and went to the interview. Although I was nervous, I didn't show it. The interview was a smashing success. The IBM manager said I'd have to earn my bachelor's degree and that IBM would reimburse me after I turned in my passing grades.

Now, I had a purpose. Instead of being debased for being "not much to look at," I was getting praised for how fast I was learning the IBM processes. I shared information with my peers, structured seminars for both customers and my other marketing team, stayed at work as late as possible to learn as much as I could, and then went to night school.

After getting my bachelor's degree, all of my grandmother's harsh (yet protective) words were no longer a part of my thinking. I rose in the company with frequent promotions. I treated people the way I wanted to be treated and never forgot my roots. I continued my education and earned my MBA.

Years later, after leaving IBM, I started my own company, was elected to three non-profit boards of directors; elected as District Governor for Toastmasters International, have written five books, and traveled around the United States presenting my etiquette seminars. I speak before Ph.D.s, corporate executives, universities and associations.

If I had let the curse of my childhood dominate my thinking, I'd probably be in a dreary life still on the Southside of Chicago. Instead, I took chances by telling myself I had nothing to lose and everything to gain by believing in God and myself.

Perhaps I should be grateful about the curse of my childhood. It made me more determined to succeed and prove Ma Peaches wrong.

I suppose every curse does, indeed, have a blessing.

Her Big But:

Sharon had every reason to let her circumstances dictate her future. Instead of giving in to negativity, she was determined to live a better life than anyone believed she could. She didn't let her big 'but' get in the way; she allowed herself to dream bigger, to take chances, and now she's living a purposeful, fulfilling, successful life.

What can you do today to help someone realize their potential?

She Has A Big 'But'!

Jean Bailey Robor

CHAPTER 3
JAN'S STORY

"Go confidently in the direction of your dreams. Live the life you have imagined."

Henry David Thoreau, poet

A common question put to young people and students is: "What do you want to be when you grow up?" If a child has a parent who is successful or that he admires, many times the child follows in the parent's footsteps and chooses the same career.

I can't remember, as a child, what I might have wanted to do when I grew up. It was a day to day existence with my parents trying to figure out where the next dollar was coming from. Our family's income put us into the poverty level. My father had a fifth grade education and he was only able to obtain laborer's positions. Feeding and caring for our family took a great deal of ingenuity. My mother, although having more education, aspired to be a wife and mother. It turned out she excelled at her goal. She baked, cooked, sewed, preserved food, and cared for ten children. Three of my siblings became special needs children as the result of childhood diseases.

I remember distinctly learning to read. What a delight the stories were to me. They took me away from my home circumstances where I answered "The Call of the Wild" with Jack

London and traveled the Orient with Pearl S. Buck.

As a fourteen-year-old student, I was introduced to creative writing by Philip Ruffner, my English teacher. It seemed I was good at weaving a story. A light bulb went off in my mind. *Perhaps, I could make a living by becoming a writer.*

The excitement over the discovery of my ability to craft the written word was exhilarating. When I had my interview with my guidance counselor, she was less than thrilled. She suggested that, while it was a nice idea, I might want to try something else. "You will never make a living as a writer. You should probably just go into the business field and do accounting or office work. You'll probably just get married anyway."

My dream was shattered. I'd never be able to do what I really desired. I'm sure the counselor looked at my family background, and she decided what she thought was best for me.

Over thirty years sped by, and yes, I did marry and have three beautiful daughters. I worked in the business field for most of those years. I forgot about my dream to be a writer. But after all, why would I even think about it? It was impossible. Wasn't it?

During those years of working, management recognized my ability to compose letters and detailed the job of correspondence and press releases to me. But other words became so insistent sometimes in my mind that I had to write them down in the form of poems and stories. I never considered, however, offering any of my writing for publication. The stories were for my husband and children.

After the last company that I worked for went bankrupt, I suddenly found myself near retirement age, and without a job. My husband Frank suggested I should write the life story of our 99-year-old friend. I could sell it for a TV movie, and we would become rich, and he could retire too. Right? *Perhaps not.*

I knew nothing about trying to have anything published. But Frank encouraged me to attend a writers' conference. It was there I met strange people (writers) just like me. We all had a dream of writing for publication. They encouraged my efforts. I guess you could say that when I returned home from the first conference, "I hit the ground running."

I wanted to make up for lost time for all the years when I could have been honing the craft of writing.

I formed a writers' group for support, and I attended numerous classes at seminars and conferences. I began to believe that perhaps I could become a published writer.

> "I began to believe that perhaps I could become a published writer."

I discovered America is a nation of opportunity and second chances, no matter what your age. I began to make my dream of becoming a writer a reality.

One of my first acceptances was a Christmas story for an anthology publication supporting the March of Dimes. The next item was a devotional for an online company for which I was paid my first commission. From that time on there was no stopping me.

In the past eight years, I have been published hundreds of times, and continue to receive payments, awards and prizes for my stories, poems and articles. I also had the privilege of writing the life story of a poverty stricken WWII Navy veteran who found America the land of opportunity as well. After his Navy service, he succeeded in business beyond his wildest dreams and became a millionaire. I felt honored to be chosen to write his story. In addition, I have two books of devotionals published, an historical fiction novella and a children's book.

My writing career evolved into a speaking career as well, as I promoted my books. I enrolled in various speaking and story-telling classes. I discovered that I also have knack for preaching, teaching and storytelling. I am now receiving payment for speaking at religious organizations, schools, libraries and civic groups.

The dream of a poor little fourteen-year-old girl to become a writer has come true.

Will I retire soon? No! I'm having way too much fun doing what I always wanted, and I'm getting paid for something I enjoy.

"Only in America can a guy from anywhere, go to sleep a pauper and wake up a millionaire."

–Jay & The Americans

Well, maybe I'm not a millionaire yet, but there's always that made-for-TV movie I'm still working on.

Her Big But:

Jan had listened to the negative advice of others rather than listening to her own heart. However, her dream, though dormant for awhile, stayed alive and she recaptured it. She didn't let her big 'but' get in the way; she realized success as an author, professional speaker and storyteller. Today, she's living her dream!

What can you do today to encourage someone to rekindle their dream?

She Has A Big 'But'!

Jean Bailey Robor

CHAPTER 4
SANDRA'S STORY

> *"At the end of the day,*
> *no matter what happens,*
> *I am blessed."*

Janet Harllee, Christian speaker

I cringed inside at his touch, knowing better than to show my disgust. I knew I shouldn't feel this way. After all, I'd been taught that marriage was forever and the man was the head of the household and that meant obedience at any cost. And he was my husband.

What I heard but not processed, in the church's teaching, was that the man had a responsibility too. To love his wife as Christ loved the church. If I had considered it, I would have realized how wrong our husband-wife relationship was. I would have realized that I was putting his will before God's will. I would have realized I didn't have to live this way. After all, Christ gave himself, his life, so that we might be saved. That's real love.

But I'd never known 'real' love. At least not in the arms of a man. Not even in the arms of the man who had promised to love, honor and cherish me 'til death do us part.'

What had happened? In the beginning, back when we were teenagers, love seemed to flourish. We were crazy about each other! He was an athlete and I was quiet and shy and admiring. He liked that about me, my admiration of him. In fact, he had told me so. "*I'd rather know you admire me than love me.*" I'd thought that a bit odd, but over the years had come to realize that it was true for him. And so I had done my best to fill that need, that need that probably stemmed from some childhood neglect, from some lack of attention.

Apparently, or so I assumed, my love, my admiration had not been enough for him. He never seemed satisfied; never seemed happy. Oh, there were moments of happiness, but always an underlying current of discontentment. "*I'm going out for awhile,*" were words I had come to dread and despise.

I couldn't understand, would never understand, why he needed anyone else when I was right here, by his side, to give him whatever he wanted, whatever he needed. In fact, I had lost my sense of self so deeply in my desire to please him that I didn't know who I was anymore.

Not only that, but I had gone way past my own moral boundaries in an attempt to please him, to keep him from leaving, from finding someone else who was smarter, prettier, sexier. In the end, I had many regrets, regrets of compromising my own values.

It started slowly.

First, he 'needed' the men's magazines. It seemed to be a burning need that would come on him every so often. And what did I know of the male breed? Maybe they were all this way. Maybe a woman, no matter how devoted, was just not enough. So, I looked the other way when he brought them home, the 'Penthouses' and 'Playboys.' A few days would go by, he would tire of them, throw them away and promise there would be no more. Empty promises.

Now I knew. Now I knew he'd had an addiction, an addiction that was just as real as if he'd been an alcoholic or drug addict. Even if I had known back then, what good would it have done? Would he have gone for counseling? Probably not. Even when our marriage was unraveling and I begged him to go to save it, he stubbornly refused.

Yet, prior to that, when the magazines were no longer enough, he somehow convinced me that sharing our bed was okay. After all, he'd said, as long as we both consented, there was nothing wrong with it. By this time my self-esteem was so low, he could have convinced me to do almost anything in order to hold our marriage together. After years of only talking about it, of reading about it in magazines, he now wanted to make his fantasy a reality.

And I complied.

After each encounter, I felt dirty, unclean. Not only my body, but to the very depths of my soul. I convinced myself that this was my lot in life. That I was not good enough to even dream of a better life. That this was how it had to be. So when our so-called 'friends' came to our house, I willingly complied. And if I seemed less than enthusiastic, I would get a harsh tongue-lashing later, another blow to my self-worth.

First I hurt. I hurt with a pain so deep and so real, I felt it within my chest as I choked back the tears. "*So this must be what it feels like, a broken heart.*" Then, I became numb. It was as if the girl I once was, the beautiful delicate flower, had wilted.

On the outside, I seemed fine. My friends and co-workers never knew anything was awry. I was too ashamed to share my pain with anyone, not my friends nor my pastor. Not just embarrassed, I was afraid of what might happen if word got back to my husband; he was a vengeful man and it wasn't easy to endure his wrath. Besides, it wasn't just my husband who had sinned. Now, I was a party to it, too. I felt like two people. One that was respectable and responsible that I showed to the world; and one that was dirty and despised that I kept hidden.

Many were the nights that I curled up under the covers and cried myself to sleep, feeling that raw painful ache in my chest. I longed for my husband to love me, to honor me, to cherish me as he had promised many years ago.

I prayed for God to make everything right. Many times it seemed my prayers were not just unanswered but unheard. And many were the times I wanted to end it all. But for the grace of God, I would have. I would have done anything to end the pain, to find relief.

> "I prayed for God to make everything right."

Finally, my world caved in. I realized that no matter what I did, no matter what lengths I went to, this was not the life I wanted to live. This was not the life my Creator had intended for me to live.

'Brave' is the word some choose to describe me. But I don't fit that description. Even after I left the relationship, after the divorce papers were signed, the battle inside me raged on. I had loved him, really loved him, despite it all. And my love ran deep. While he'd once held tightly onto me—more as a possession than a loved one—now he let me go, without a fight. The realization of how little he must have truly loved me hurt the worst.

I had given up myself for nothing more than this?

Today, I am living a life I love. I'd like to tell you that it happened overnight, that the pain is gone, that I've been set free. I'd like to tell you that, but it would be a lie.

Instead, my truth is that, while I have been set free and while I do love my life, there are obstacles that I've had to overcome to get here. And there is pain that still raises its ugly head from time to time. And, the peace didn't come overnight, but through a period of years.

It's not something I'd want to experience again, but I would if that's what it took to get where I am now. I'm fortunate that God put key people and opportunities in my life. He'd probably been doing that all along but I was too hurt, too blind to see. Once I opened my eyes and began to look, I found ways to raise myself up, to build my self-esteem, to get involved in my community. And when I focused on helping others, my own hurt didn't hurt as much. The healing: it's a process. My prayers are being answered, not in my way, but God's way.

Her Big But:

Sandra was in a toxic relationship. Low self-esteem and bad choices could have been her reasons for failure. However, she didn't let her big 'but' get in the way; instead, she put her faith in action, moved forward, embraced opportunities and is living a life she loves.

What can you do today to show someone the possibilities of living a joy-filled life?

She Has A Big 'But'!

CHAPTER 5
CICI'S STORY

"*Life is either a daring adventure or nothing.*"

Helen Keller, author & lecturer

I received a phone call. It was her. I was busy running errands, and this was my last stop and I just wanted to go home, eat my Chinese food and snuggle in to the recliner while everyone else was out of the house and just,…well,…you know…BE. EXIST. NOT BE NEEDED. NOT EVEN BY THE DOG.

But, as I got out of my car and stood on the sidewalk, knowing that my conversation was about to be weird at best and I couldn't go in to the restaurant until the call was finished, my plan for a quiet evening dissolved.

Came the voice on the other end: "Whatcha doin'? Got a minute to talk?"

My fake smile hopefully went out over the phone as genuine, "Sure! What's up?"

"Well, I really wanted to talk to you for a minute about….about…..dating."

Really? Did I need this now? Was life not just hard enough today without having to talk about one of the biggest topics between relatives? The conversation continued. "Well, you know that it has been a long time since we talked about dating, and I actually think I am ready now. To date, that is."

Of course, I did the old 'pregnant pause'.....oh, no.....did I say *pregnant*? I found a brick wall to sit down on outside the restaurant. This one was gonna be one of *those* conversations.

I weakly replied, "Go on. Tell me more." All the while I wished the call would drop. No such luck. What a time for my cell phone carrier to be reliable.

"Well, I really like him and I saw him at Bojangles and he sat down to talk to me because we had met before at a party and he asked me out and I said yes. So, can I? Do you think it's OK? I promise we will be home early."

Lightning was now flashing inside my eyes. My mind went blank for a second. I realized that the inevitable was happening.

Quick thoughts ran through my head...what about this guy and his family? Do I know him? Is he the kind

> "I realized that the inevitable was happening."

that might get "frisky" with her and lead her into sex before she's ready? What about HIV/Aids? I had just read an article about these things occurring more in her age group than any other right now.

Not only was I feeling upset about my evening being ruined with this great decision weighing heavily on my mind, but I could see my future filling up with sleepless nights, worry and dread. Great. Just when I get through one season of parenting, here comes another.

So, what should I say? "OK, dear. If you think it's time, then I'll go with it."

About a month after they began dating, I got another call. "Guess what? He gave me a ring for my birthday!"

You know those lighting flashes I told you about...you know, the ones inside my eyes? They now went dark, and I sat down quickly on the floor, since I knew that passing out from shock would lead to my meeting with the floor somehow, some way. I actually got out a word in response.

"WHAAAAT?!?"

"Oh, just kidding." She laughed. No, she actually giggled. "It's just a birthstone, but it's soooo beautiful!"

Now entered the anger stage. "Look here, missy, don't EVER do that to me again! My heart can't take it!"

She said, "But what if we did decide to get married? Wouldn't that be OK?"

Immediately, "Uh, NO! Have you lost your mind? Please tell me you are not serious, because, at your age, you shouldn't even be thinking of marriage. Please tell me that I am not going to get a call from Vegas that you guys eloped. Please!"

"Oh, no, I won't do that anytime soon. I mean, really." She lowered her voice. "Besides, I know that I just met him and we need to date longer before we do anything like that. And his daughter feels the same way that you do."

"Daughter? Daughter! How old is this guy, anyway?" I was mentally calculating the low and the high age, and I got goose bumps on top of goose bumps. Could it get any worse?

"Well, he's only 4 years older than me, and I know that we need to take caution."

She did say "caution" and not PRE-caution, right? My mind was not processing well. The lightning flashes were back in my eyes again.

"OK, tomorrow we are going to talk, just you and me. I am going to tell you about S-E-X and the incidence of HIV/Aids in your age group, and you are going to listen. Until then, nothing happens, promise?"

The next day at work, I relayed the story to my lunch bunch. The comments I got were NOT helping me. "Aww, isn't that cute?!" "Hooray, for her – she's dating!" "You go, girl! Tell her it is wonderful!"

Incredulous yet again, I retorted, "That's not the sentiment I was hoping for from my friends! What is wrong with you? My mother has been widowed just a couple of years, and she is acting like a 17-year-old! Not only am I parenting my teenage daughter, I am parenting my parent, and it stinks! After all, mom's 81! And who would like to go along with me when we do the S-E-X talk, hmmmmm?"

I paused. Silence. "Yeah, that's what I thought. See, it's not so cute anymore, is it?"

Well, I'm happy to say that I have at least one friend on my side. She had endured the same thing with her mom and she gave me great advice: If she acts like a 17-year-old, treat her like she is 17, and remember:

- Don't expect her to show up at any family functions for awhile.
- Don't let her sign any legal documents at this time.
- Don't expect anything she says to make sense.

Since that day, I have not had to carry around paper bags to breathe into, because I am not having anxiety attacks anymore. And since that day, I have learned more than I ever thought I would about "The Dating Game in Your Eighties." And don't worry – if or when your time comes to explain all that to your mom, remember, I've been there and done that.

And survived.

Her Big But:

Cici was in-between, having a teenage daughter and a mother on the dating scene at the same time. She found it challenging that her mother had chosen to date, again. She didn't let her big 'but' get in the way; instead, Cici realized that everyone needs close relationships and she chose to help her mother, just as she'd helped her daughter, address the concerns/issues in today's dating world.

What can you do today to demonstrate compassion to someone whose actions are hard to understand?

She Has A Big 'But'!

Jean Bailey Robor

CHAPTER 6
TIFFANY'S STORY

"You can change the world as long as you believe it is worth changing.

I do."

Angel Guerrero, Change Agent & President, AS Web Pros

On Tuesday, May 29, 1979 at 4:00 PM, a child was born out of wedlock to a prostitute. I heard stories that the birth father was an engineer, married with children; he was Puerto Rican; the mother was African American. This made it doubly hard, especially when people would ask, "Where did you get that white baby?" While others considered her pregnancy shameful, little did they know someone bound to do great things had just been created.

That someone was me.

After 13 hours of hard labor, I was born with a clubfoot. For three months I was forced to wear a cast on my left foot. Prior to my birth, my mother had not picked out a name. Once she saw me, she gave the name Tiffany, the highest quality of jewels one could purchase. To her, I was a diamond. She thought I would be her ticket out of poverty and Tiffany "the diamond" would make her life better than everything she had ever dreamed of. My mother had a hard childhood. As the oldest of seven children she had to give up her dreams to take care of her siblings. Not only that, but her childhood was filled with physical and verbal abuse. I remember her telling me how her father was so cruel to her mother, even burning her with lit cigarettes and once punching her so hard her head burst open. This scared my mother so much, seeing her own mother lying on the floor, bleeding.

Her father not only physically abused her mother but their children, physically and sexually. Since she never received the proper help she needed to deal with that, she repeated the cycle of abuse. Because she had suffered at the hands of those who supposedly loved her, she grew up to think that if a man didn't beat her it meant he didn't love her. Abuse, to her, had become a way of life. A way of life that she unwittingly passed along to me.

Besides prostituting to earn a living, mother became an alcoholic. That meant, she wasn't always there, physically or emotionally. And she often was not aware of all that went on in our home. Not that it would have mattered; she was too broken and bruised to care for her own self, much less her child. But there were moments where she tried. She was a wonderful seamstress and made all our clothes.

From time to time, she had moments of wisdom. Once when, as a child, I stood outside my elementary school, sad, she asked what was wrong. I said, "I wish you were white." I just wanted us to be the same. This must have hurt her but she put on a rare smile and said, "Tiffany, no matter what color we are, we are beautiful."

There were also times when we would play board games on a Sunday afternoon and life seemed 'normal.' Then the bad would begin all over again.

At age 6, I began to be sexually abused on top of the physical abuse. I cannot begin to tell you how worthless I felt, how my heart was broken, how I cried so many times in my misery. This continued until I reached the age of 16.

I couldn't take it. At the first opportunity, I left home, vowing this would be the last black eye I would endure from the woman I called "Mommy."

I didn't have the capacity of making the best decisions. I just knew I wanted out. I moved in with my boyfriend. He was very controlling, jealous and mentally abusive. I realized I had gotten out of one bad situation and into another. I decided to leave.

Again, the grace of God spared my life.

> "Again, the grace of God spared my life."

I believe I overcame these adversities because of my faith. Plus, I believe God had given me an inner strength and I had a deep desire for something more. As I grew, I began to watch the people that entered my life. People who took me to church; people who showed me what living above their circumstances was all about. God brought these key people into my life that believed in me and wanted to see me succeed. I paid attention and committed myself to learn from them. I also learned what I didn't want from people that were not so positive. Because of my past, it would have been easy to follow the path of least resistance and stay grounded in my environment, living beneath my circumstances. Instead, I had a strong desire to succeed and, over time, I began to move in a positive direction.

Because of that, I've been blessed. I've been married for more than ten years now and I'm the mother of two brilliant young men. Today, I am a successful entrepreneur, inventor, designer, healer and motivational speaker, encouraging others to tap into their potential.

I've broken the cycle of abuse and I'm loving my husband and my children the way God intended. My boys have made me proud in becoming chess champions of our state for three consecutive years. As a result of my journey from a life of heartache to a life of joy, I wrote *Dare to be a Diamond* in hopes that my life might be an inspiration to those who have experienced or are experiencing similar life events.

Perhaps, my mother did see some potential in me, way back when she named me Tiffany. Like a diamond that shines only after many years of pressure, I was bruised over and over again, and I've come out shining.

Her Big But:

Tiffany had every reason to fail. She was battered, abused and hurt, not just physically but emotionally too. She could have easily given in to her circumstances, yet she didn't. She didn't let her big 'but' get in the way; instead, Tiffany rose above her circumstances and now, through her writing and speaking, helps others do the same.

What can you do today to help someone rise above their circumstances and live a life worth living?

She Has A Big 'But'!

Jean Bailey Robor

CHAPTER 7
JOANNE'S STORY

"The sense of independence and security is very sweet."

Susan B. Anthony, American Civil Rights leader

To say I had low self esteem would be an understatement. Ever since junior high school, I can remember that I never felt good enough. I tried everything I could to get noticed. Somehow, I felt that other people's opinions of me mattered more than my opinion of myself. I decided to do something; something that would really get me noticed. And maybe, just maybe, if other people admired me, I would feel good about myself.

While some of my classmates partied, I studied hard and it paid off. I became the valedictorian of my class. Surely this would give me the attention, the admiration I craved. Surely, it would make me feel good about me. However, it wasn't long after I achieved that, I realized that it didn't give me the feeling that I thought that it would. As you can imagine, I was very disappointed.

While setting goals and achieving them was never a problem for me, realizing that I was "worth" it was. I kept looking outside myself for that validation. And I found no satisfaction. No matter what goals I reached or how high I achieved, I still felt empty.

However, I realized through much research that the validation I sought had to come from within. What a startling, yet true, realization. I began to comprehend that by listening to the negative self-talk in my head, I understood why I felt the way I did. My thoughts controlled how I felt.

> "My thoughts controlled how I felt."

Slowly, I began challenging those thoughts in my head and realized that my thoughts aren't who I am. Today, I stay vigilant of my thoughts and challenge the ones that don't seem valid. Consequently, I can choose what reactions and actions that I can take toward a situation.

For many years, because of my low esteem, I was in "reaction" mode. I reacted to everything that happened and interpreted events negatively. I never realized that I had the power to control how I thought or reacted to situations. I realize now that I have the power to react positively to events and interpret them how I want to interpret them.

My moment of success was when I realized that I didn't have to believe the negative thoughts in my head. Once I really came to grips with that insight, I knew that I didn't have to react to events around me.

And I didn't have to allow other people's thoughts or actions control my actions.

Today, I lead a happier, healthier lifestyle. I rest in the knowledge that whatever I pursue, I do it because of how I feel about it and about myself. If others admire me for it, that's great. But, if not, I don't let it bother me.

I'm comfortable in my own skin.

Her Big But:

Joanne, an intelligent, successful student did not have confidence in herself. Because of her low self-esteem, she set goals to please others rather than looking inward for validation. However, she didn't let her big 'but' get in the way; instead, when she realized she could enjoy a happier, more fulfilling life, she took the initiative and never looked back.

What can you do today to build confidence in a young person and help them see they are a beautiful creation?

Jean Bailey Robor

CHAPTER 8
BETH'S STORY

Jean Bailey Robor

> *"Not all of us can do great things. But we can do small things with great love."*
>
> Mother Teresa, humanitarian

It wasn't a matter of thinking, *It'll never happen to me.* Instead, I never thought of it at all. When I was a child, my mom was invincible. When I became an adult, I began to understand more about her as a real person, someone whose health often dictated her involvement in life. Even when I was young, she led a sedentary lifestyle. But she was always there to read to me, help with homework, show me how to cook a favorite dish. If I wanted to play ball outside, dad would take over.

Still, as I entered mid-life and I watched as her health declined, I never considered my role in her future. I was too busy focusing on my own children who were in their teenage years. Just as the last of them left for college, it happened. Mom began falling from time to time. For no apparent reason. Later she was diagnosed with neuropathy[2], a disease that can cause pain and numbness. Over time, her legs were affected to the point she needed to walk with a cane to steady herself. Two years later, she had

---

[2] Neuropathic disorder often associated with diabetes.

graduated to a walker. Still, she would fall occasionally. As her daughter, someone who loved her, I couldn't bear the thoughts of her injuring herself. So far, she had only suffered bruises, but what if she fell and broke a bone?

By this time, dad had passed on and mom was living alone. We lived within 5 miles of each other so I visited with her several times a week, took her shopping and to doctor appointments.

"You shouldn't be living alone," her doctor informed her. I'd never thought about making decisions for my mom, especially a decision of where she would live. She was Ms. Independent, taking care of all of her affairs much better than I ever could. But when faced with the news that she needed to live somewhere she could be cared for, I saw uncertainty in her eyes. And for the first time, for this woman who had cared for and protected me, I felt protective of her. As her only child, I began to feel the responsibility. I remembered the times she had cared for me, the times she continued to love me, in my rebellious teenage years, when I was unlovable. And I knew there was no way I was going to let her down.

On the way home, she and I discussed the conversation we'd had with her doctor. She really didn't want to move out of her home, out of the place she and dad had lived together last. There were many memories there, good ones, and she held onto them, relived them, enjoyed them.

After she'd had her say, I told her I felt she should move in with us. I wanted to keep an eye on her. After all, if she fell, she couldn't get up on her own. What if she fell and laid there for hours before we found her?

We decided to compromise. She would live with us during the week and stay at her home on weekends. She would keep her cell phone with her at all times so we could check in with each other. That worked for awhile until her health declined further and that's the part I'd never thought of at all. What would happen when mom needed a caregiver?

Somehow it seemed only natural that I would fill that role. I'd never had any training in caregiving, and, often, the long days would get the best of me. By now she had graduated to a wheelchair. Loading and unloading it was no piece of cake for this middle-aged woman. I'd find myself feeling angry, then guilty from feeling angry. Who was I angry at? Not mom;

she couldn't help her situation. And besides, I loved her! Still, each day it seemed I was losing more and more of my joy.

One day, when I loaded up the wheelchair and took her to the mall, we passed other women, other reluctant caregivers. I saw their stooped shoulders, their dull eyes. And I knew that was me. When my kids would visit, I could see, hear their concern. Had I let the long hours of care pull me down? I was no longer the girl with the positive attitude that mom had raised. Who had I become?

"I knew I needed something but I didn't know what I needed."

I knew I needed something but I didn't know what I needed. So I went to classes for caregivers to find out how to do it better. I learned how, as people age, they become more sensitive, bruise more easily and her neuropathy caused her pain in the simplest tasks. And yet, she never lost her positive attitude. In many ways, she was still the mom, teaching me by example, to be joyful even in bad situations. Still, I just wasn't getting it.

In the classes, I also heard how easily caregivers can burn out, how they need to take time for themselves, how they shouldn't feel guilty when they take that time away. I learned that I needed to care for myself so that I might care for her better.

And that's when I began to regain my spark. Occasionally, I took time to go shopping on my own or with a close friend. I would enlist the help of my children or home health aides to stay with mom while I took a mini-vacation, a half day of doing whatever I wanted to do. At first, I did feel a measure of guilt, even though my mother encouraged me. But I found that when I fed my spirit, I cared for her more joyfully and it raised *her* spirits. In fact, I would hear her on the phone with her friends talking about how she enjoyed our time together. And I would smile, my heart warmed. Anytime I found myself going through the motions, I knew it was time to plan a little outing again. Plus, having new and different faces around, new people to talk with, seemed to rejuvenate mom's spirits as well.

Of course there were times when those little outings were few and far between. As mom's health waned and her hospital visits became more frequent, I knew I needed to be right by her side. If you've ever had a loved one in the hospital, you know what that's like. It's easy to become both emotionally and physically exhausted. But I learned that when mom's friends would visit, I could slip away for a bit, even if just to take a walk outdoors and my spirits would lift. And still, even in her hospital room, she set an example, telling little jokes to the nurses to lift their spirits and asking them about their day, their families, their dreams. Even though I wasn't a child, I would always be her child, and she was leading me, teaching me how to live.

I learned to step outside my busy-ness and find joy in the simple things, like walking in the park, reading in the quiet of the library, writing poetry in a coffee house, lunching with friends, having a 'date night' with my husband. I regained my life all while serving my mom better.

We began to share those special moments of love and laughter more often than we had in years. By allowing myself to feed my soul, I found I could bring more joy into her life. The time we shared was sweeter than ever before.

Today, while I never saw it coming, I wouldn't trade that experience for anything as I'm now an advocate for 'reluctant' caregivers, those family members who found themselves in a situation they never expected to be in. After caring for mom, while I don't consider myself an expert, I did learn a few things along the way. So I encourage others, the way I was encouraged, to find ways to get away for a bit and revive their spirits. And I often see hope spring anew as their eyes light up.

I'll never forget, after speaking to a women's group, how one woman, Jill, came up to me with tears in her eyes. After some conversation it was clear; she was caring for her dad and was so like me 5 years ago, when my light began to fade. She grasped my hand and held it, warmly, as she spoke, "Thank you for sharing your story. You've given me hope."

A month later, Jill was a new woman, as I found when I opened a letter addressed to me: *In the same moment I felt like giving up, God sent you my way and showed me that life can be filled with joy. I just had to choose my path. Today, my dad and I are both happier. Because of you.*

It still amazes me that I can make a difference. *Mom, you taught me well.*

Her Big But:

Beth found herself just going through the motions. She knew she should care for her mother and she wanted to, no question, but she didn't know how to do it joyfully. She knew something had to give. She didn't let her big 'but' get in the way; instead, Beth sought out classes for caregivers and put what she learned in action. She reclaimed her own life and made her mom's life better in the process. Today she shares with others the importance of self care in order to care for others better. And she shares how they can make it happen.

What can you do today to rejuvenate your spirits, feed your soul, revive the joy in your heart?

Jean Bailey Robor

CHAPTER 9
YOLANDA'S STORY

"One tiny ray of light can brighten the darkest room. You can be that ray of hope!"

Marilyn Pergerson, educator

In July of 2000, I suffered a minor heart attack, but . . I didn't let it slow me down. In September of 2001, I suffered another. In September of 2005, I was diagnosed with type 2 diabetes, but . . . I didn't take it seriously. In May of 2006 I suffered a mini-stroke.

Women have always been innovators and 'nourishers' of the earth and I was no different. Even though I was divorced, I was successfully raising two children on my own. In addition, I was working full time at a stressful company and ran my own business full time. I had always been the picture of good health and never really had any health issues besides allergies and the minor cold. In 2000 my mother had been diagnosed with brain cancer, and after I had my first heart attack, my doctor told me that I needed to slow down, because if I didn't the stress would surely kill me. But . . . of course I didn't listen, after all, I had things to do and an entire world to conquer.

I came, I conquered, and I then I had another heart attack. My doctor put me on medication and continued to warn me. Had I not been ignorant to my situation, I would have taken the time to find out my family's history. For, had I done so, I would have found out that my family genealogy harbored a host of health issues, including diabetes and high blood pressure.

In September of 2005, as I sat at work drinking my daily Sonic Strawberry Fruit Slush, I fainted. It was then that I was diagnosed with type 2 diabetes. My mother had diabetes before she died, my father had diabetes before he died, and my grandmother has diabetes. She has had it as far as I can remember and yet she ate anything she wanted, whenever she wanted. Currently, she is a feisty 80-year-old, so if she could go on about her life, why couldn't I?

I continued about my life as if the diabetes diagnosis hadn't happened, as if the two heart attacks hadn't happened and even as my weight began to increase, I chocked it up to my busy lifestyle and not being able to find time to exercise. Smokers, alcoholics and drug users say they can stop whenever they want. I knew I could lose the weight, whenever I wanted. That was until one day in May of 2006 when I tried to get out of bed in the middle of the night to use the rest room and fell from my high sleigh bed, flat onto the floor. I couldn't feel my right side and I couldn't speak—it didn't matter, I lived alone, no one would hear me.

At the time, I had no idea I was having a stroke. I didn't know what was going on. Luckily, my doctor had convinced me to get a Life Alert system. I had fainted several times before and had experienced what it was like when the fire department knocked down your door to come to your aid. Doctors say it is extremely important for a stroke victim to seek medical care within the first four hours of a stroke in order to limit the damage.

I had no idea how much time had passed from the beginning of my stroke to the time it took for the fire department to knock down my door. Again. I gather, had I not had been awakened by my urge to use the rest room, I may not have lived to share my story.

But, shortly after my stroke, I endured weeks of speech and physical therapy, at which time my doctor told me that he might have to take my leg.

"It was at that point that I really began taking my illness seriously."

There was a lot of nerve damage. It was at that point that I really began taking my illness seriously. Right before my stroke, I had taken on a second job, in addition to the two I already had, to pay for a nice big house in the suburbs of Dallas, Texas. I quit my part-time job and ran my business on a part-time basis. I started taking my meds and my insulin regularly, joined Weight Watchers® and starting making more informed and healthy decisions on what I ate. In addition, I started working out on a regular basis and began removing those things in my life that proved most stressful. I knew that if I wanted to continue to conquer the world I could not do it if I was dead. But . . . I have to admit that I didn't follow my doctor's regimen 100%, but I was on the right track.

In November of 2007, my fiancé moved me from Northern Texas to the Piedmont Triad area of North Carolina. Then as my new husband, he did all he could to make sure my stress level was as low as possible. I found a job working at a medical practice, but . . . my heart wasn't in it. I still had some conquering to do and I couldn't do it sitting behind a desk pushing papers.

In January of 2009, I quit my office job and decided to take my business full time. I began marketing and networking and building up my contact base and I'm happy to say, I am currently working on my fourth novel and business is pretty good. I was determined that I was not ready to leave this earth yet. I have too much unfinished business. I know in my heart that God has the final say so as to what will or will not happen in my life. And I believe that while I am here, I will continue to serve my purpose. I make sure that my loved ones are aware of the importance of knowing their health history.

Recently I attended a book signing of a fellow colleague, friend and bestselling author. During her discussion, she mentioned my name. Several people in the audience gasped and said, "That's that author. That's *That Literary Lady!*" I was known by some and that touched my heart more than anyone could ever know.

This winter, I will be penning a non-fiction book about my diabetes journey, a children's series and a Christian mystery series.

I'm happy to say I no longer have a big 'but.'

Her Big But:

Yolanda's stress had escalated to the point it was affecting her physical health. While she was involved in good things, she was over-extended, and it was taking its toll. Not only that, but she had never taken the time to discover her family health history. She found a way to get her big 'but' out of the way. Yolanda began to take her health issues seriously and make lifestyle changes and encourage others to learn their family medical history. Plus, she re-examined her priorities and focused on what was most important, the dream that God had given her.

What can you do today to take a step toward living your dream and helping others live theirs?

She Has A Big 'But'!

Jean Bailey Robor

CHAPTER 10
CANDY'S STORY

"If you take a bit of time for yourself and for your dreams, you will feel more alive in every single area of your life."

Sheila A. Steplar, author, *Journey 2 Joy*

If you look at me now, you'll see a bubbly, self-confident and successful woman. But life wasn't always this way. And each time I share my story to help others, I put a little more of the past behind me and I feel stronger. I'll start at the best place to start, the beginning.

My mom and dad began dating when they were fifteen. They were high school sweethearts. Everything was wonderful at first, but young love can also be the hardest to keep. They were both tempted to drink as teenagers and my dad became an alcoholic.

Still, they loved each other. But to complicate matters, mom became pregnant at eighteen. They decided to get married and a few months later, I was born.

Dad found it hard to settle down. He ended up making some bad choices which landed him in prison for several years. So, at 23 years old, mom filed for divorce and became a single mother of three young children.

We all ended up living with my grandparents. In our new home, my grandparents showed us lots of love. In the absence of dad, Grandpa became a father figure to us. From time to time, Dad would come into our lives, then he'd be gone again. Mom never took him back.

We lived a strict Christian life. We were all expected to go to church. It was not an option. Mom put the fear of God in me at an early age. I can remember being a pre-teen and worrying about whether or not I was going to die and go to Hell.

Even so, I enjoyed church. I was a good girl. It was my brothers who rebelled at a young age. It seemed that Mom was always worrying about them. After school was out, they would not stay home and she would have to look for them throughout the neighborhood.

She didn't have to worry about me. I mainly did as I was told. I often felt that my mom overlooked me, because she was always concerned about my brothers.

My school life wasn't great. I was skinny, had asthma and acne. I was treated by some people like I wasn't good enough. I didn't live in a nice house, wear nice clothes and I wasn't popular. I was a late bloomer. The girlfriends that I did have were true. Most of the boys overlooked me. Plus, I was shy, which didn't get me anywhere socially either. A part of me always felt like I just didn't fit in.

At the age of sixteen, I started hanging around a group of friends who had dropped out of school. They drank, but I didn't. After only seven months, the peer pressure became too great and I found myself sucked into their behavior.

One night, a boy poured a little bit of wine down my throat. I drank it. I could have stopped right then and determined that I wasn't going to drink. Instead, I chose the opposite path. I said to myself, "Why not?" After all, after that incident, I couldn't claim that I'd never tasted alcohol.

It was a very bad decision. It wasn't long before my drinking spiraled out of control. I didn't know when to stop. I would black out. I would do things out of character. I would get sick often.

Life began going downhill fast back then. I also didn't realize that alcoholism can run in families. Both of my brothers were faced with the same problem. One started drinking at thirteen and another at sixteen. Interestingly, we had all chosen the same path, separately.

Because my self-esteem was so low, I began dating rough guys who treated me badly. I was so desperate for love that I would take whatever I could get. I would spend money on these guys, thinking that they would eventually care for me more. Every relationship was a disaster. It wasn't love.

I continued drinking off and on. I was fun, flirty and the life of the party. I would say and do things that I wasn't proud of but I couldn't seem to control my behavior. It was like I had a split personality. I was the good girl sober and a wild woman when I was drunk.

I dropped out of church right after I started drinking. For months at a time I would be sober but always ended up going back to the bottle. I found out later that I was a binger drinker. I was my own worst enemy. I ended up with a bad reputation and my self-worth hit rock bottom.

Most of my friends would tell me that I needed to quit or slow down. Even my friends that drank. That was how bad it was. I ended up making a promise to God that if He would help me get my life together that I would quit drinking. When I made that promise, I really meant it, yet I only stayed sober for six months. Then, on top of everything else, I had a lot of guilt for not keeping my promise. I would tell people not to stand too close to me, because I might be struck down any minute, for breaking a promise to God. I wasn't joking.

I believed it.

My irresponsible behavior escalated. I quit paying my bills on time. I continued to spend lots of money at the bar and on my guy friends. I worked two jobs and still struggled financially because of bad choices. I felt out of control and unsure about what the future would bring.

I knew in my heart that I would quit drinking when I got older. That's what I told myself. I didn't realize that it would be so hard to quit. I was so unreliable that my car was repossessed for not making my payments. I had to pay a large fine to get it back. I was demoted at my job and practically bankrupt. I knew I had to change, but I wasn't sure how to change.

That was the beginning of my real struggle to get sober.

It would take years.

I had reached the end of my rope and I knew it. I went to counseling for bad relationships. I didn't know why I always wanted guys who were unstable. I guess their neediness made me feel wanted.

To my surprise, my counselor told me that I needed substance abuse counseling because of my drinking. I had been drinking two to three times a week. I was proud and didn't believe that I was a true alcoholic. The word

> "I was proud and didn't believe that I was a true alcoholic."

'alcoholic' didn't even sound right coming out of my mouth. I knew that I could quit. I told her that I would quit on my own if she would counsel me. She said that she would.

I believe it was just what I needed to help me change. I just didn't know how long it would last. After all, I had quit before but always went back. She told me not to quit drinking for her but to quit drinking for myself. I told her that I was doing it for me. It felt good to be challenged.

Little did I know that decision would change the rest of my life. I wasn't making anymore promises to God. I just asked Him to help me get through each day and I would try my best to stay sober. That was it.

I actually thought that being sober would solve all my problems. I was wrong. I had to face the reasons why I was drinking. I needed help with codependency with men and my lack of self-worth. In the beginning, I had bad mood swings, depression and the temptation to drink was strong.

After the first three months, I was able to think clearer. I learned that it takes years to fully get over the effects that alcohol has on your brain. The fog lifted a little bit.

I knew I had a long way to go. I set a goal to make it to the first year. I wanted to get my chip at AA[3], even though I seldom attended the meetings. I had gotten back into church and attended services three times a week. I was

---

[3] Alcoholics Anonymous- a fellowship of men and women who share their experiences, faith and hope to help others recover from alcoholism.

trying to get the relationship with God back that I had lost so many years ago. My life changed tremendously. I lost most of my friends because I wasn't drinking with them anymore. Now, we hung out in different places. Sometimes when I did hang around with my old friends, I found I was tempted to drink. It was hard.

But I made it! To one year! On my one year anniversary of sobriety, I chose a random AA meeting to attend. I stood up and got my one year chip[4]. When I left that evening, a man walked out of the building with me. He asked if I was truly an alcoholic. I admitted that I was.

To this day, people still question me. It feels good to know that I don't still look and act like

---

[4] Some AA groups give chips to commemorate years of sobriety.

an alcoholic. My Dad and brothers still drink. I have talked to them over the years about quitting. They say they don't feel normal being sober. While that may sound strange to some, I know what they mean. It takes a long time to get comfortable in your own skin after becoming sober.

I've been sober for ten years and I couldn't be happier. I am glad to be me. It was a hard road, but I made it! I've also learned to treat myself a lot better. My relationship with God is better, but I know I'm not perfect. I learned to accept my flaws. I am in a good relationship with a man who truly loves me.

The best advice I give to others who are in a situation similar to mine is not to give up. I drank for twelve years before I finally quit for good. Just take it one day at a time and if you fail, get up, dust yourself off and try again. I would still be drinking to this day, if I had not tried that one last time. If I can do it, I know others can do it, too.

Her Big But:

Candy's self destructive behavior, coupled with alcoholism, led her down a path of hurt and disappointment. It almost destroyed her life. However, she didn't let her big 'but' get in the way. Instead, each time she failed, Candy chose not to accept the failure and to get up, dust herself off and try again. Ten years later she enjoys a successful life.

What can you do today to get past what's holding you back and move toward your goals and dreams?

She Has A Big 'But'!

Jean Bailey Robor

CHAPTER 11
CLAIRE'S STORY

*"For God has not given us a
spirit of fear, but of power, and
of love and of a sound mind."*

2 Timothy 1:7 NKJV

I didn't want to live. One morning, I had dropped the children off at school. I was nervous. I'm not even sure I kissed them good-bye. I drove to the next town where I would go into court to finalize a painful divorce that had been a long time in coming. A few short hours later, I found myself a non-custodial parent. And it hurt like hell.

I remember when they were young. I was a stay-at-home mom, spending hours reading to the children, taking them to the playground, hosting sleepovers for their friends. Life was good! My husband was in the military and it seemed that times were happier when he was away. When he came home, he would often get angry with me and the children for the least infraction. I felt like I was walking on eggshells. So, even though I loved him, it was easier to love him from a distance.

Living on the military base was the best. There were women, just like me, married with children whose husbands were away frequently. And we formed close bonds. Even closer than the friends I had made at a local church off base. The commonalities we shared included being away from our extended families. We became each other's sisters, mothers and friends. We shopped at the commissary together, pushed our babies in their strollers together, and kept the peace among the kids.

Once my best friend, Amy, and I decided to take on the task of waxing our vehicles. Neither she nor I had done this before and we saw it as a challenge. Plus, my minivan certainly needed some attention! We purchased all the supplies, pulled out the hoses and went to work, washing and scrubbing our vehicles to get them sparkling clean before putting on the wax.

The children thought it was such fun, splashing in the soapy suds and squirting the vehicles—and each other—with the hose. Once we began the towel-drying phase, they soon lost interest and Amy and I were left on our own to slave away in the hot summer sun while the children danced around a nearby sprinkler.

Then the waxing began. Somehow, I hadn't thought of how I would reach the top of my van to wax it. She hadn't considered that either. At my height, or lack of it, it was all I could do to reach the top of each side. Then Amy had a bright idea. A step ladder! I followed her to her storage building and we hauled the stepladder over to the parking area.

She didn't know this, but I had a fear of heights. I also had some pride so I didn't admit my fear. I just climbed on up there and began to apply the wax, trying to calm my racing heart with positive affirmations. Still, try as I might, I couldn't reach the center of the top of the van, not unless I climbed on top of it. And that wasn't going to happen!

I looked back at Amy. She was happily waxing her compact car. There wasn't a spot on it that she couldn't reach. It was going to look great once she wiped the wax off. Mine, on the other hand, if I didn't come up with a solution, was going to have a dull streak a foot wide across the top.

I considered it briefly, then decided it wasn't worth stressing over and, besides, who was going to be able to see it anyway? So, I left it.

A week later my husband returned from his deployment. As usual, he would inspect and criticize everything from the house, the yard, to my personal appearance. This time was no different except that he noticed the shiny-ness of the van. At first he was

> "I still remember the look he gave me and the harsh words he said."

pleased, until his detailed inspection revealed the dull streak on the top. I still remember the look he gave me and the harsh words he said. That was 20 years ago. To this day, I've never waxed another vehicle.

After he decided to leave the military, we moved back to our hometown. By now, two of the children were in school and the youngest would begin the next year. Things between us were a bit better. It probably helped that we had family around. Grandparents, aunts and uncles took time with the children, taking them to movies, the park, out to dinner and for an occasional overnight stay. Life was good.

Over time, life became not so good. Financial challenges caused more stress which gave way to anger. I began to be afraid of my husband and what he might do as his verbal abuse gave way to physical abuse. I would lie in bed at night, crying, helpless, as he took off his belt and went upstairs to discipline the children. Today it's hard to imagine that I didn't fight back. But then, I was a different person, very dependent and with low self-esteem. I didn't have the emotional or physical strength to go against him. His control was so strong, oftentimes just a look would keep me and the children in line. To say I was without fault would be a lie. I should have stepped up and voiced my opinions. I should have taken some action. Many times. Maybe if I had, we could have gotten help and worked through this. But, instead, I remained silent.

Finally, I could take it no more. My heart was breaking, not just for myself but for our children. By now, all of them were in school.

I filed for divorce.

Because of what I had cited in the divorce papers, my husband came to me, after his anger had assuaged, claiming he was afraid he would be put in jail. I still loved him and it wasn't hard to convince me to call my lawyer and stop the process. Still, I didn't want to go back to the way it had been and we agreed to a separation agreement.

To say he was manipulative would be an understatement. Somehow, he convinced me that, as we had only one son, he would be better off having a father figure around. Else, who knows what kind of man he would grow up to be. Even though I knew he wasn't a good father figure, I found myself convinced it would be the right thing. So I agreed for our son to live with him and he agreed our daughters would live with me. It would be amicable and we would get together with the children frequently. And, who knows, maybe one day we would get back together and have the fairy-tale relationship I'd always dreamed of.

Little did I know that the entire time he had plans to take away my most precious treasure. He intended to sue me for custody and take away all my children forever.

That's how that, by the time a year had passed, I found myself sitting all alone in the courtroom, waiting for our divorce to be granted and a custody decision to be made. As I sat there, I was beaten down, broken, and I prayed silently. I didn't know if my prayers were being answered or not. I had grown disillusioned with God and the church, even angry, for what He had allowed to happen. The breaking up of my family. I couldn't see that it wasn't God that destroyed it, but us.

So while I sat on one side of the small courtroom, my soon-to-be ex-husband sat on the other side, with his family and his new girlfriend.

My lawyer came in late, which didn't help matters. Especially when the judge asked me where he was and I had no answer. When he did come in I found out that the kids had been picked up from school and would be taken into the judge's chambers one at a time. While we waited, they would tell him, through their tears, that they wanted to live with their father.

After the two oldest had been taken in, my lawyer said he had never seen anything like it. He described how distraught they seemed. I had to do something. I had to stop them from being traumatized. Before the youngest went in, I advised my lawyer to stop it. The only way I could make that happen was to agree to joint custody with the children being placed in his home, over 50 miles away.

I did it.

I know that if I could go back there now as the strong woman I am today, things would be different. I also know that there is no turning back and regrets only hold me back from moving forward. It's taken me years to realize this. And today, as I write these words, I feel the ache in my chest and the tears on my face; the hurt is just as real now as it was then.

Being a non-custodial mom isn't easy. I'm more convinced than ever that marriage should be forever. That we should fight for our families and do everything that's possible—counseling—before giving up. In a perfect world, we'd all have those perfect families. The mom, the dad, the well-behaved kids. But this isn't a perfect world and we reap the consequences of bad decisions. Still, I know now that God can be in any circumstances, that He does care. It's taken me a long time to realize that.

On that day, after court, I went home. The house felt empty. For years after that, I couldn't go into the children's rooms without crying. Even when they would visit, the thought of their leaving put a heavy cloud over most any happy times we experienced.

My heart broke, daily.

I knew I couldn't live like this, but, as much as I thought I would welcome death, suicide was not an option. Over time, I realized that, as painful as this was, this was not the end. My children were still alive. And somehow came the realization that I needed to be an example for them.

So, after years of looking only inward, feeling my own pain, I began to look outward, to see what I could do, what I could say to make their lives better. Once I did that, I felt better too. I had a purpose.

I reclaimed my relationship with God and found a support group for non-custodial moms. Their stories broke my heart yet brought us close. We wept together when things weren't going well and we rejoiced when one of us regained custody. I found that there were other women who felt, just like me, an outsider at our children's ball games and school functions. I found that they, too, saw the disapproving looks of others when they were brave enough to admit their children did not live with them. I found other women who, because of an unfair court system, had lost their children and now lived thousands of miles apart, unable to even enjoy every other weekend together. I found non-custodial moms who had been unfairly accused of child abuse and were required to have supervised visitation.

And while I saw this happening to non-custodial mothers, I wondered how often it happened to non-custodial fathers.

But there's a stigma attached to non-custodial moms; it's almost as if being 'non-custodial' is the same as being labeled 'unfit.' People wonder why a mother doesn't have her child in her home. *Is she a drug addict, an alcoholic? Did she neglect her children? What's wrong with her?*

For awhile, I didn't get too close to people because I was ashamed to admit it, even though I had always treated my children with love and care. Then there were times when I acted as though it was a joint decision because, living with their dad, they were in a better school district; it was better for the kids.

Sooner or later, I found, that you have to accept the truth and that the truth, as hard as it is, will set you free.

Today, the children are grown and we are closer than ever. There's no doubt of the love we feel for each other and for the God that healed our hearts and made us whole. Still, we don't talk about that time. It's too painful. Instead, we focus on the now and on the future, all the exciting things that can and will be.

And we can do that, by the grace of God.

Her Big But:

Claire could not see past her own hurt. For years, she harbored anger and resentment and allowed it to rule her life. Only when she took her eyes off herself and onto her children did she begin to heal and help others in the process and get her big 'but' out of the way. Today, she enjoys a successful life, helping others who are hurt by life's circumstances to rekindle their dreams.

What can you do today to look through the eyes of non-judgmental love and ease another's pain?

She Has A Big 'But'!

CHAPTER 12
MARTA'S STORY

Jean Bailey Robor

"Act as if what you do makes a difference. It does."

William James, philosopher

She stood before a leadership team in a large corporation. It was a planned presentation, one she had prepared for during the past month, one she had anticipated with enthusiasm. Yes, she was nervous but she'd been told that a little nervousness kept you on your toes.

Having given many presentations in the past 8 years, she knew this to be true. However, just as she was about to be introduced before this crowd of her peers and her management, Marta's mind drifted back to a time 14 years earlier.

She was quiet by nature but involved in a family retail business where she dealt with the public each day. It helped get her out of her shell a bit to meet and greet and problem solve. Still, she was more content curled up on the couch after a long day with a good book.

Within a few years, the business she was in began to fail and she started looking elsewhere for employment. A friend recommended a large corporation which was headquartered nearby. Marta visited their Human Resources department and browsed through the book of job openings. So many to choose from. And so many that wanted someone with a 4-year degree, something she didn't have.

Marta was a college dropout.

She wasn't proud of it and had always intended on going back to school but then she and her husband started a family, then she began working outside the home, then….. life just got in the way.

> "Life just got in the way."

She applied for 17 entry level positions that day. Interviews were scheduled for two. One job was offered to her. She took it.

Time passed by. Children grew up. Marta realized if she was going to live a successful life, she would have to venture further out of her shell. She chose to work on her self-esteem and confidence. She joined several organizations where she met new friends, networked and began to grow. After years of giving to her family, she now found time to give something back to herself. And in doing so, found a freedom she'd never known. And a passion for public speaking that she'd never even dreamed of.

Marta has been promoted several times within the company. She's taken classes to further her education. She gives hope to others through her presentations to church groups and corporations. The first time the Vice President of a leadership team sent her an encouraging note after she gave her team a motivational talk, it brought tears to Marta's eyes. And, with all this, she still finds time to curl up on the couch and read a good book. But now, more often than not, it's a book about becoming better at what she does and then there's the occasional novel. The once-shy little girl has grown up and into a more confident woman than she ever believed she could be.

And there she stood. Ready to take the stage. As she was introduced, following a long list of accolades, Marta took a deep breath, stepped forward and began to speak.

One of her coworkers leaned over to a colleague and said, *She has a big 'but.'* In fact, she had several. Low self-esteem. Little self-confidence. A lifetime of shyness. She had overcome them all to be here, in this moment.

Her Big But:

Marta used her shyness as an excuse to hang back and watch life from the sidelines. Eventually, she took charge of her life and proactively sought out ways to help boost her confidence and change her life. She didn't let her big 'but' get in the way. Today, she is more confident than ever and is enjoying a joy-filled life.

What can you do today to propel yourself forward both personally and professionally?

Jean Bailey Robor

CHAPTER 13
TAMMY'S STORY

"The best way out is always through."

Robert Frost, poet

My early childhood memories are littered with feelings of insecurity. I can't completely explain why. My mother was supportive and loving, proudly taping my earliest artwork on the refrigerator, and saving my first attempts at writing poetry. My father sensed that I was a "tomboy" (or perhaps shaped me to be one) and I was constantly at his side – hunting, fishing, working on cars, and making household repairs. Yet he was a very anxious person, who was irreversibly scarred from his experiences in WWII. I was born with the desire to make others around me happy, and I wonder if my inability to "fix" my father's unhappiness spawned my insecurity in my overall abilities.

Regardless of the reasons, I was always unsure of myself. I double and triple checked everything I did, sure that it wasn't up to par. Basically, I painted myself into a corner of self-doubt that tattooed everything I thought of attempting. This even applied to the thing I loved most – writing. Still I *had* to write. It wasn't just a desire; it was a part of me. I had a diary before I started elementary school. It was very pretty, with gold-trimmed pages and a strap with a lock and key. I wrote little poems in the diary, and more often than not, the entries were short on fact and long on the fictional concepts that I loved.

My mother nurtured my desire to write. I absolutely *loved* words. When the Reader's Digest arrived, I immediately opened it to the feature *It Pays to Increase Your Word Power.* I would turn to that page and study each word, trying to guess what it meant. I spent what seemed like forever choosing my answers. Afterwards, my mother would check them. I was so proud when I answered correctly, and promptly proceeded to torture my family by using these newfound words as often as possible.

As I grew up, I continued to write, mostly poems and short stories. Of course, journaling in my diary was always a part of my everyday life. Still I wanted to write more. In middle school, the creative writing portion of my English classes was my favorite. I received high grades, but still I didn't feel that what I had written was really *that good*. During my high school years, writing was a large part of my life. My stories and poems were filled with the angst so common in the life of a teenager. Again, my grades were very good, and my teachers were complimentary, but I only viewed those compliments as the grading of an assignment. I never considered them to be an indicator of whether or not I could be a good writer.

After high school, life took over, and my writing took a back seat to marriage and motherhood. For many years, I wrote nothing more than my journal entries, many of them splattered with baby food and formula stains.

Still, I wrote. It was a part of me, but more and more, a secret part. The further I moved from the judgment and advice of teachers, the less sure I was of my own ability. I no longer had a way to measure my work, and eventually my insecurities won out. I kept my writing private. No one knew about the stories and poems I wrote, not even my family.

Many years later, in 2004, the local library began an "Open Mic" program. This program consisted of monthly meetings which allowed the attendees to read their own poetry. For quite a while I waited and wondered if I should dare to take my notebooks full of poetry to one of these meetings. I am, by nature, a shy person. The thought of standing in front of a group of people to read my own words, some born from very personal life experiences, was terrifying. There were times when my insecure self would intrude when I considered attending a meeting:

Why in the world do you think your writing will be good enough for others to hear? Don't you know they will laugh you out of the room?

These thoughts were strong and persuasive, and for quite some time, on the night of the meetings, I would wait until the last minute, only to decide to stay safely at home.

Then, a little spark inside of me began to grow. I had an idea. My sister is an avid reader of poetry, and she is very vocal about her opinions of what she reads. She and I often share poetry that we enjoy, and we like similar styles. What if I sent my poetry to my sister, with no author credit? What did I have to lose in using her to test my writing? Eventually, that is exactly what

I did. I sent two carefully picked poems to her, attached to an email. Then I waited anxiously for her to write back with her critique. A couple of days later, I saw her response in my email inbox. I was surprised at how nervous I felt, but this was after all, what I had asked for. I opened her reply and when I saw her words, I was shocked. She loved the poetry, making references to specific phrases, styling, and most importantly, she wanted to know who wrote the poems so that she could read more of the author's work! I replied very simply, "I wrote them."

Within two or three minutes my telephone rang. It was my sister. "You wrote these?" she shrieked. "Why didn't you tell me you could write like this?" I admitted that I wasn't really sure if they were good or not. Her response brought me to tears. "Are you kidding? These are great! You have to get these published."

Armed with the confidence of her honest reply, I began to submit my poetry to various publications. Of course I got plenty of rejections, but I was also published, and frankly, I was surprised, but I was getting braver. I finally attended an "Open Mic" meeting, and there I met Jean Bailey Robor, the woman who would become my best friend. We chatted before the meeting began, and found that we worked for the same employer, and of course, we shared our common love of writing. When my turn came to read, I thought I was literally going to die – or pass out. Either way, I wasn't sure I could get up in front of the group and read my work, but

> "When my turn came to read, I thought I was literally going to die – or pass out."

I did it. An amazing thing happened when I concluded my reading. People clapped! When I returned to my seat, Jean said, "That was great!"

Since that day, my walls of insecurity have disintegrated. To date, I have co-ghost-written several books, ghost-written an autobiography, written book reviews for a local newspaper, many articles for local magazines and various newsletters. I also wrote a children's book, published a book of poetry, taught a mystery writing class and am currently working on a novel. I owe so much of my new-found confidence to my best friend, Jean. She is my support, my editor, my honest critic, and most importantly, my friend.

I often wonder how different my life would have been if I had not had a positive response from my sister and the unwavering support of my friend. I wonder if I would have conquered my fear of sharing my writing. Perhaps I would have in time. Perhaps I was already pushing against the wall I had built around my creativity and only needed someone there as I pulled out the first brick I had stacked up.

Most importantly, I've learned that life is too short to waste by being mired in self-doubt. The time I wasted can never be retrieved, but now I can be true to myself and trust in my abilities. The personal rewards I have gained are immense, and I am so happy that I'm finally free to express myself through writing – my greatest pleasure in life.

Her Big But:

Tammy lacked confidence in her abilities even when others praised her. Somehow she just could not believe she was good at almost anything she tried. Finally, a break-through came when someone unwittingly praised her poetry and she began to believe in herself. She didn't let her big 'but' get in the way. Today, she continues to enjoy her passion, writing, and has the confidence to write for and share her writing with others.

What can you do today to follow your passion?

She Has A Big 'But'!

Jean Bailey Robor

CHAPTER 14
LAURA'S STORY

> ## *"All I have seen teaches me to trust the Creator for all I have not seen."*

Ralph Waldo Emerson, poet

I was angry. Not just angry but, like my dad would have said, mad as a hornet. I had gone out back to my garage to get the lawn mower. Cutting my lawn was way overdue. I frowned at the tall grass in the back. The last time I had begun cutting it we'd had a thunderstorm so only the front yard had been trimmed. Now, after a couple of weeks, the back was beginning to look like a jungle. So, reluctantly, I donned my tennis shoes and went outside to mow.

When I entered the garage I noticed my lawn mower was gone! Someone had stolen it. I stood there for a moment, feeling the anger rise within me. It made me angry that someone would come into my yard, into my garage and steal from me. Besides that had been my favorite lawn mower. It was nothing fancy, a Briggs & Stratton push mower, self-propelled and the cool thing was, you could start it with a key. I loved not having to pull on the cord to start it.

Now, someone had come and walked away with it. And I was not happy.

As the anger churned within me, I remembered a few weeks ago when our Wednesday night growth group had a discussion on anger. It was definitely timely. Now I could put what I'd heard into practice, to keep my anger under control.

I wasn't known for having anger issues; I never let it get out of hand. But at that moment, I really wanted to punch someone, the person who had stolen my lawn mower. I was sure that would make me feel *so* much better.

Then, as I walked up the driveway, I began to see God at work. I felt as if He was showing me His handiwork. As if He knew what was going to happen ahead of time (which He did), He had prepared me. For one thing, the growth group discussion was timely. Plus, I had recently received an unexpected financial blessing equivalent to three times what the lawn mower cost. God was taking care of me. It just took me awhile to 'see' it. And I thought to myself, "They can steal my lawn mower, but they can't steal my joy!"

> "They can steal my lawn mower, but they can't steal my joy!"

By the time I made the police report, my heart was actually light. I was no longer angry. I was beginning to realize that while I was going to miss that mower, I really had not had enough time to keep the lawn trimmed the way it should have been. This was one of the busiest years in my business.

And I began to wonder, maybe that lawn mower was, right now, being a blessing to someone else. Maybe to the person who bought it, not knowing it was stolen. And I also began to wonder if maybe the guy I'd just called to mow my lawn for the rest of the summer needed the work more than I knew. Maybe he had a family to feed and was struggling.

I smiled as I tucked an extra $10 in the envelope with his quoted fee.

Maybe all my 'wonderings' were just my way of keeping my anger at bay. Or maybe they were somehow true.

On the other hand, I chuckled, maybe my lawn mower left of its own accord, because it wasn't getting enough of my attention.

Naaaa......

Her Big But:

Laura found anger festering inside her heart. But, because she saw God's hand in her less-than-perfect situation, she found joy. She didn't let her big 'but' get in the way; instead, she chose to thank God for preparing her ahead of time, even when she didn't realize it.

What can you do today to dispel your anger and turn an otherwise ugly situation into something beautiful?

Jean Bailey Robor

CHAPTER 15
MICHAELA'S STORY

"Too often we underestimate the power of a touch, a smile or the smallest act of caring, all of which have the potential to turn a life around."

Leo Buscaglia, Ph.D., author

She was born in Yonkers, NY on the majestic Hudson River. Before she met and married her life-long sweetheart, she was an editor, accomplished linguist of several languages and management consultant. It seemed that after graduating with a degree in French and holding positions in both New York and Paris, success was just around the corner.

She met Augusto, an Italian economist, in Milan and life became even sweeter as they pledged their love to each other and were betrothed. Augusto said it was love at first sight "with her delicate beauty, natural elegance and remarkable blend of spirituality and human warmth, Michaela was a very attractive woman, in fact quite irresistible."

In Washington, DC, On May 29, 1978 they were blessed with a beautiful dark-haired baby boy. There was no way they could have known that in a few short years, they would be involved in the fight of their lives that would span decades.

From the beginning, Lorenzo was a curious child who hungered for knowledge. And Michaela was all too eager to give it to him. By the time he was 5, he was fluent in English, French and Italian. His kindergarten teachers spoke well of him, noting him as precocious and bright. Michaela and Augusto could already see Harvard in his future.

Soon Augusto's position with the World Bank took him to the Comoros Islands in the Indian Ocean, a French-speaking island-nation. Michaela and Lorenzo went with him. She ran an informal clinic which distributed medicines donated by U.S. charities. According to Augusto, "She had a history of helping people in their moments of need, especially the poor and disadvantaged."

Michaela enrolled their young son in French classes, expecting him to excel as well as he had back at his school in the States. Instead, Lorenzo's teachers reported that he had a short attention span and he began to have behavior problems, highly out of character for their young son. Soon, they noticed he was having problems with his eyesight. Michaela wondered if he had contracted a tropical disease but doctors soon ruled that out. Even so, Lorenzo's hunger for knowledge never wavered.

> "Lorenzo's hunger for knowledge never wavered."

They enlisted the aid of a private tutor and, even as Lorenzo's eyesight failed, he found pleasure listening to stories of the Greek myths and the music of classical composers such as Bach and Handel. Studies in math, history, geography and literature provided him a well-rounded education.

As Augusto left for work each day, Michaela watched, helplessly, as her bright young son's health continued to deteriorate. By the time he was 6, Lorenzo began to experience blackouts and lapses in memory, his speech became slurred and his behavioral problems worsened. Some physicians and psychologists believed he was brain damaged. But Michaela remembered her intelligent little boy and was unconvinced. By now he was beginning to lose his hearing. She took him to specialists and, eventually, a brain scan confirmed that their son suffered from ALD[5].

---

[5] Adrenoleukodystrophy- A rare progressive degenerative disorder that affects the nervous system due to a lack of myelin.

The diagnosis was devastating. After doing some research Michaela found that once diagnosed, most ALD patients live only 2 to 3 years. That meant her son would not see 10 years old. The worst part was that, with such a rare disease, no one was doing research to find a cure.

Augusto and Michaela had to do something. Although they weren't of the scientific community, they contacted medical professionals and scientists, desperate to find some help for their little boy who was slowly sinking into a vegetative state. They were met by some with disdain; others tried to discourage them and said it was pointless to try to fight the disease and that Lorenzo would live two more years at best. However, that did not deter them. With the support of Hugo Moser, a neurology and pediatric professor from Johns Hopkins

University, they eventually discovered a treatment now known as Lorenzo's Oil. Unfortunately for Lorenzo, the discovery, while it prevented further regression of the disease, could not completely restore his health. However, it did take him from an almost vegetative to a responsive state. But for others, when diagnosed early enough, it had the potential to prevent patients from experiencing the same devastating effects to their nervous systems.

Michaela, relentless, was by her son's bedside for up to 16 hours a day, making sure he was fed the oil through a tube. She also made sure he was dressed during the day and dressed for bed at night. They had a special chair made so he could sit up and scheduled a regime of massages, exercise and physiotherapy. Eventually, they moved to a bungalow and set up his bed and other necessary equipment in their main living room where he would live out the rest of his life attended round the clock by either his parents or nurses.

"We never entertained, never travelled, never took vacations," recalls Augusto. Michaela's sacrifice for Lorenzo wore her out. She taught him to communicate by blinking his eyes and wiggling his fingers. And he remained curious, intelligent. Dr. Moser, later discovering a blood test to detect ALD in newborns, admired the dedication of both parents, "They will stop at nothing to restore Lorenzo. How can anybody criticize that?"

With their discovery, Michaela and Augusto Odone saved lives and made medical history. And the care plan she created for Lorenzo has been praised by all doctors familiar with the case. Their story is recounted in the 1992 film, Lorenzo's Oil, in which they were portrayed by Susan Sarandon and Nick Nolte. Michaela wrote a poem, *Lorenzo*, which was set to music and performed by Phil Collins. In it, she recalled memories of her beautiful little boy when all was well:

Down on Grand Comoro Island, where I grew past four; Well I could swim and fish and snorkel on the ocean floor.

Michaela continued to care for Lorenzo as he grew from a boy into a man in their Virginia home even after she was diagnosed with lung cancer. By now, she and Augusto had grown close to Hugo and drew great comfort from his friendship. He was one of the few who did not question them for wanting to keep their son at home. Michaela, knowing her time was short, made recordings which Augusto would play for

Lorenzo after her death. She was ever the loving, dedicated mother to the end.

Because of the relentless quest and constant care by Michaela, the little boy who should have died before reaching age 10, lived until 30.

Today, Augusto Ozone lives in Italy and continues to be a driving force to combat ALD through the Myelin Project, a charity he and Michaela founded which promotes research into diseases which destroy myelin[6]. The intent is to bring hope to those that suffer from conditions such as ALD and multiple sclerosis and other leukodystrophies. The spirit of Michaela, a woman who often jumped into situations to correct injustices and right wrongs,

---

[6] White matter of the central nervous system which is needed to transmit messages from the brain to other parts of the body.

lives on. In the words of Augusto Odone, "If during her earthly life Michaela touched the lives of countless people, her legacy of commitment, love and compassion will continue to be an inspiration to parents of sick children for years to come."

Her Big But:

Michaela saw her perfect family challenged when her son became ill. Once diagnosed, she was discouraged, even by medical professionals. However, she didn't let her big 'but' get in the way. Instead, she became more determined than ever to do everything in her power to save her son's life and, along with her husband, extended his life and may have saved thousands of others.

What can you do today to make a difference in your home, your community, your world?

Get Past your Big 'But'
with Jean Bailey Robor

<u>FIND YOUR JOY</u>

"This is the day the Lord has made;

let us rejoice and be glad in it."

– Psalm 118:24

Have you ever thought how wonderful the day would be if you lived by this premise? To rejoice, to be glad in the day. To simply feel the joy of living. When I make a conscious effort to enjoy the day, I truly find myself having a better day than if I let my circumstances dictate my day. You can do this, too.

Joy truly is a choice. We can't always control situations we find ourselves in but we can choose how we react to those situations. Many times, if we simply choose joy over sadness, victory over defeat, love over hate, our entire mindset will be so much more positive, more satisfying.

I remember when I was a child. I could hardly wait for the next day. It was a pleasure to hop out of bed and into a new day. The days were filled with possibilities, with anticipation of spending time with my friends, playing outside in the fresh air, making new discoveries. I found joy in the simplest things: finding a smooth stone, chasing a butterfly, fascinated by lightning bugs. How about you?

What happened? How did we lose our joy? Did we let life's circumstances get in the way? Did we allow other people's opinions to steal our joy? Did we, somehow, acquire a big 'but'?

Do you have a big 'but'? Something that's keeping you from experiencing true joy? Something that's holding you back from your dreams?

Choose today to move closer to the joy-filled life that awaits you. To anticipate each new day with child-like wonder. Let's rejoice and be glad in this day the Lord has made!

<u>FIND YOUR INNER PEACE</u>

"My peace I give you…
do not let your hearts be troubled."
— John 14:27

Have you ever hungered for peace? Peace in the world, in your family, peace of mind? We were created to experience peace, to let our hearts not be troubled. To lay our heads on our pillows at night and welcome sweet, peaceful rest. When I embrace the peace that only God can give, I rest well. On the other hand, when I'm worried about the cares of the world, I don't rest so well. What about you?

Having peace in our hearts is achievable. First, we have to change our way of thinking. It's only natural to focus on our problems, on the things that cause us stress. We have to consciously turn our focus toward the things that bring us joy, that calm our hearts, that are positive. So much of it depends on us.

I can remember times when I've failed at focusing on the right things. There were nights when I tossed and turned and had a terrible time getting to sleep *(and that was before menopause)!* I would worry and fret over situations and circumstances, many which were beyond my control. Now, am I saying we should keep our heads in the clouds and not face reality? No. But I do believe we have opportunities to experience peace of mind and we fail to take advantage of those opportunities. Somehow, we've acquired a big 'but'.

Do you have a big 'but'? Are there cares and concerns that are keeping you from experiencing true inner peace? Is your focus on something or someone that is holding you back?

Choose today to take God's Word at face value. Don't allow worries to overshadow the peace that your Creator can give. When stressful situations come your way, take a moment to breathe deeply, clear your mind of worry and focus on the positive. Let not your heart be troubled!

FIND YOUR LIFE

"This is my comfort … for Your word has given me life."
— Psalm 119:50

Have you ever felt the pain that comes from a broken heart? Have you ever felt that you were alone? Have you ever dreamed for a better life but didn't know how to achieve it?

When we experience heartache, disappointment and pain, we can find comfort in the arms of a loving God. People, while some are well-meaning, will often let us down. God will never let us down.

When I read Psalm 119:50, I rest easy in the knowledge that my comfort can be found in the realization that He has given me life. Whatever life it is, I should live it according to His glory.

Do I do that? Every day? No. I'm as human as anyone. I'm nowhere near 'perfect.' I don't always persevere through hard times and come out shining and I don't always make the right choices. And when that happens, God is still there. He is a God that gives second chances and offers forgiveness freely. And I kinda like that about Him!

Finding your life means taking stock of where you are now and where you want to be. If you look closely, you'll find that you have a God-given desire, God-given talents. You were created for a purpose.

When I look back to where I've been and where I am now, I can see God's hand in it.

When I think of my future, I know He's there. And I know that today, He is preparing me for what's out there. He can prepare you, too.

The best way to find our life is to loosen our grip on our life and give it over to Him, to trust Him. That may mean finding a Bible-based, faith-filled church. It may mean searching the scripture for direction. It may mean hanging out with new friends who will build you up and encourage you rather than tearing you down. It may mean, stepping out in faith to reach others in a way that only you can reach them.

There's no better day than today to put your painful past behind you, look toward your future and celebrate your life.

Let this be your comfort, *God's word will give you life.*

And you don't have to start from 'perfect.'

FIND YOUR DREAM

"If you can believe, all things are possible."
— Mark 9:23

Have you ever thought how wonderful life would be if you could truly believe that all things are possible? Now you can.

When we live our lives the way our Creator intended, we can rest on the promise that all things are possible. Does this mean that we'll get our every desire? No. Just like our children come to us with wants that we don't fulfill for their own good, our Heavenly Father does not give us everything we want for our own good. Sometimes we can't see that. We just have to trust. But I believe that God puts desires in our hearts that he wants us to fulfill. I believe He gives us a dream and then he makes a way for us to make it happen.

I can relate closely to some of the women whose stories are in this book. I remember when I first recognized my dream of writing. It began in the 5th grade when our class was given an assignment to write a poem. I had never written a poem but had enjoyed reading the little nursery rhymes, the limericks, sonnets that were in the books stacked beside my bed. I carefully constructed my poem, *Little Girl,* and read it in class the next day. It was about a family's trip to the beach written from the perspective of a young girl. I was shy and nervous and, honestly, that teacher really intimidated me. But on that day, she praised my poem, which was not great by any standards. Her praise encouraged me so much that I began to write more and haven't stopped yet!

Interestingly, like many young writers, I had often thought I'd write the great American novel, but, through the years, my writing has taken a different route, at least for now. It's just one part of my life that has become a dream realized.

Can you identify something in your life, a desire in your heart that you'd like to move toward? Look for opportunities to make that dream a reality. God doesn't put dreams in our hearts to lie dormant, but to become something great, something giving, something fulfilling.

Believe.

All things are possible.

SOURCES & RESOURCES

These sources include resources for you on your life's journey plus references to the admirable women and men who contributed to this book.

Bailey Allard, President, Allard Associates, Inc.
www.baileyallard.com

Michael Geffner, award-winning writer/journalist

Henry David Thoreau, poet

Janet Harllee, Christian Speaker/Entertainer,
Songwriter, Storyteller
www.janetharllee.net

Helen Keller, author & lecturer

Angel Guerrero, Change Agent & President, AS Web
Pros
www.aswebpros.com

Susan B. Anthony, American Civil Rights leader

Mother Teresa, humanitarian

Marilyn Pergerson, educator

Sheila A. Steplar, author, *Journey 2 Joy*
www.thejoystream.com

William James, philosopher

Ralph Waldo Emerson, poet

Leo Buscaglia, Ph.D., author, University of Southern California professor

Jim Tudor, President, Tudor's Total Effect LLC
www.tudorstotaleffect.com

Sheryl Roush, author of *Sparkle-Tudes*® and *Heart of a Woman in Business*
President/CEO, Sparkle Presentations, Inc.

Sharon A. Hill, President, Sharon Hill International
ABETA Certified American Business Etiquette Expert
www.sharonhillinternational.com

Jan Sady, professional speaker/storyteller & author:
God's Lessons from Nature, God's Parables and Lessons, Book 2, Sacagawea, The Bird Woman, The Great American Dream, Mr. Bernie's Most Favorite Place
janfran@windstream.net

Tiffany Anisette, CEO
Tiffany Anisette International LLC

Joanne Tudor, Student Success for Life
www.studentsuccessforlife.com

Yolanda M. Johnson-Bryant, author, professional speaker, literary consultant, social media specialist
That Literary Lady
www.yolandamjohnson.com

Robert Frost, poet

Candice Dickson, public speaker

Tammy Hall Shropshire, author, freelance writer & friend

Michaela & Augusto Odone, founders
The Myelin Project
www.myelin.org/

Find additional help:

Alcoholics Anonymous- www.aa.org

Dave Ramsey- For sound financial advice, programs & products, www.daveramsey.com

Focus on the Family- A global Christian ministry dedicated to helping families thrive.
www.focusonthefamily.com

Heath Evans Foundation gives the sexually abused a voice at www.imavictim.com

To search the Bible- www.biblegateway.com

Special thanks to all the brave women who contributed their stories and wished to remain anonymous.

She Has A Big 'But'!

Jean Bailey Robor

ABOUT THE AUTHOR

Jean Bailey Robor, award-winning professional speaker and author, has an enthusiasm for life. Having overcome many of her big 'buts' she has become an inspiration for women everywhere. In addition to writing and speaking, Jean hosts the radio show *Celebrate Life!* A native of Burlington, North Carolina, she is active in her community and is instrumental in helping others see their value and achieve their highest potential. Jean believes when you take responsibility for your actions and choose to live the life God intended for you, you'll experience a successful, joy-filled life and realize your dreams.

Jean is available for book signings and presentations to church, civic and business organizations. Her passion is to encourage, motivate and teach others skills to grow personally and professionally. She lives in the heart of North Carolina with her adorable furry friend, Maxie, and a few humans.

www.jeanbaileyrobor.com

Stay connected with Jean on Facebook, Linked In & Twitter!

Jean Bailey Robor

SNEAK PEEK!

If you enjoyed *She Has a Big 'But'!* you'll want to read *She Has a Big 'But' Too!* For more information on upcoming *She Has a Big 'But'* books or to participate in the *She Has a Big 'But'* project, visit www.shehasabigbut.com.

To God be the Glory

Jean Bailey Robor

Made in the USA
Charleston, SC
09 September 2011